All new
Delicious
slow cooker
RECIPES

Simon & Alison Holst

Published by Hyndman Publishing
325 Purchas Road
RD 2 Amberley 7482

ISBN: 1-877382-66-3

TEXT: © Simon & Alison Holst

DESIGN: Rob Di Leva

PHOTOGRAPHER: Lindsay Keats

HOME ECONOMISTS: Simon &
Alison Holst, Michelle Gill

FOOD STYLIST: Simon Holst

STYLING & PROPS: Pip Spite

Introduction

This is Simon's and my THIRD slow cooker book! I suppose that I must admit that we are slow cooker addicts! If you had suggested to me, five years ago, that this would be the case, I would probably have laughed you to scorn, but now I hate to be without a slow cooker on my work bench!

"Why is this?" you may ask. Simon and I think that the best thing about slow cooking is that for many of our recipes we can put our prepared foods into our slow cooker in the morning, before we get on with all the other things we have to do during the day, then forget about it until it is time for our evening meal. Then when we come into the kitchen we are met with wonderful aromas, and feel that a good fairy has cooked the meal, and all we have to do is serve it and EAT it!

Also important, especially when times are harder than usual and we are watching how we spend our money it is good to think that a slow cooker, turned to LOW, uses very little energy (about the same as a light bulb). We also like the thought that tough, inexpensive cuts of meat will be tender and full of flavour when slow cooked.

Nothing burns on the bottom of slow cooker bowls, so we don't ever have to waste burnt food, or soak and scrape the bowl.

If you are thinking of buying a slow cooker and are shopping around, compare the different models and decide which you suits you best. For example, you may choose a slow cooker with the basic instructions HIGH, LOW, KEEP WARM and OFF, or decide that you would like a slow cooker which has automatic timing, so you can turn the cooker on and off when it suits you. Don't feel that you must have a small slow cooker if you are cooking for one or two. Most of the time I cook for two, but I usually make enough for four or six, serve one lot immediately, refrigerate the second lot, and maybe freeze the third lot.

There is an important "Don't" when slow cooking. Slow cookers heat up slowly. They also cool down slowly, so you should never leave a large mixture to sit at room temperature for longer than necessary — the food may spoil and your family could become really ill. Get into the habit of putting extra food in the refrigerator in covered containers AS SOON AS the food is at room temperature.

Simon and I hope that you will also read through the following few pages because they are really important. They are much the same as the "Before You Start" pages in Book 1 and Book 2 but they are good reminders.

We hope that you and your families enjoy the recipes in this book as much as we do!

Good cooking,

Simon and Dame Alison Holst.

Contents

Before you start slow cooking

We suggest that you read these pages before you start using your slow cooker so you can benefit from our trial and error experience.

Manufacturer's instructions. Always read the instruction booklet supplied by the manufacturer before you use your slow cooker and follow their recommendations, rather than our suggestions, if they differ.

Cooking times. Slow cookers don't all cook at exactly the same speed. The wattage of a slow cooker, details of which are stamped on the bottom of the machine, is a measure of the machine's power. Larger, higher-powered machines usually cook food faster than smaller machines of lower wattage.

Slow cookers vary. Just like electric frypans and ovens, slow cookers of the same make and model may differ slightly in the speed at which they cook. However, modern slow cookers tend to cook somewhat faster than those made 20 years or so ago. We have used new machines for all our recipe testing. Get to know your own slow cooker.

Wattage. Details of a machine's wattage can be found on the base. The machines we used to test our recipes ranged from 155 watts to 350 watts. In general, small slow cookers use less power than larger machines because they are cooking less food. Also, different brands may use different levels of power, so may cook the same amount of food in different times. With this method of cooking, "faster" is not necessarily best. We expect food in a slow cooker to eventually bubble around the edges on HIGH, but not on LOW. If you have a machine that bubbles on LOW, you will probably need to use shorter cooking times than those given in our recipes.

No mess! When you use a slow cooker, you think ahead, prepare ahead, and clear away ahead too. When it is time to eat, there is almost no mess – how wonderful!

HIGH or LOW? As a rule, food cooked on HIGH cooks in half the time of food cooked on LOW. You can change from one setting to the other to speed up or slow down the cooking. Most foods (but not dried beans) can be cooked on either setting. By doing part of the cooking on HIGH then changing to LOW, you can cook your food in whatever time you have available.

All day or part of the day? Some of our recipes call for all-day cooking. Others are intended for starting after lunch, just before children get home from school, or before you get caught up in the end-of-day toddler routine.

Crockpot or slow cooker? Crockpot was the brand name of an early model of slow cooker and, much like Biro or Hoover, the name became widely used.

Cheaper meat cuts. When cooked in a slow cooker, these are often more flavourful and tender than more expensive meat cuts. We use the cheaper shoulder cuts of lamb, pork and beef with great success. Corned brisket and silverside are excellent too. They will be ready after the minimum cooking time suggested, but will probably be even better if left for 1–3 hours longer.

Don't peek too often! When you take off the lid, the cooker loses heat and the cooking time is prolonged. When you have to check the contents, work really fast and get the lid back on again as quickly as possible.

Overcooking is seldom a problem. Because slow cookers cook so gently most types of food (but not fish, pasta, baked dishes, puddings and rice dishes) may be left for an hour or two longer than specified, especially on LOW, without overcooking.

What size/shape slow cooker? Small cookers are great for one or two people and take up little space. Larger ones will, of course, cook food for more people or enough for several meals for two people. We usually use a larger cooker because we find that refrigerated or frozen leftovers are a real bonus. A chicken, pot roast, large meat loaf, or large piece of corned beef may fit more easily in an oval cooker than a round one. On the other hand, in a large round cooker you have room to put vegetables on each side of the chicken, etc. This shape cooker also makes round rather than oval cakes.

Warming time. It takes time for the contents of a slow cooker to heat up. The ingredients for a slow cooker recipe, which have been prepared, assembled and refrigerated overnight, will take longer to heat up and start cooking than the same ingredients at room temperature. This does not matter when a 6-8 hour cooking time is involved.

Night-before preparation. If preparing food the night before, refrigerate it in plastic bags or in covered containers. Then put it into the slow cooker in the morning, and turn it on. This saves refrigerator space and means that the slow cooker bowl is at room temperature (not chilled) when you start cooking.

To brown or not to brown? Please yourself, choosing any one of the following options:
· sear meat in a pan first
· coat it with a spice or herb mixture
· brush it with dark soy or other sauce at any stage
· cook it in a colourful sauce
· leave it 'au naturel'.

Onions. Onion cooks very slowly in a slow cooker. Lightly browned onions cook faster and taste better. You can:
· reduce the amount of onion considerably, or even leave it out
· use smaller amounts, chopped finely or grated
· brown chopped onion in a frypan, in a little oil before adding to the slow cooker
· microwave chopped onion, coated with a little oil, in the slow cooker bowl until it sizzles (but only if you know that the bowl is microwave-proof).

Thickeners. Sauces may be thickened in various ways. For most people, cornflour is always on hand, but is not as efficient as arrowroot or potato starch (sometimes called potato flour). You need less of these and they thicken sauces almost immediately, whereas cornflour thickens liquids more slowly, sometimes needing up to 15 minutes' thickening time. Meat floured before browning thickens gravy slightly. Well-cooked kumara or pumpkin will thicken sauces too.

Liquid. In a slow cooker, the liquid does not boil away – you usually finish with more than you started. If you are modifying an existing recipe for a slow cooker, use about half the liquid called for in the original recipe, (except for soups!). You can also cook foods in the slow cooker with no added liquid at all, e.g. meat loaf, chicken etc. We often place food such as roast or dry-baked chicken (whole or pieces) on Teflon liners. These help with the removal of food too.

Dense vegetables. Potatoes and carrots are good examples of dense vegetables, which often take longer to cook than meat. Cut them in small same-sized pieces for even cooking. Push larger pieces (especially potato) down the sides, with the cut surfaces close to the edge, near to the base.

Easy clean-up. Before cooking, coat the inside of the slow cooker bowl with non-stick spray or a little oil. After dishing up, completely empty the bowl before standing it in the sink and filling it to overflowing with water the same temperature as the bowl with a little detergent added. By the end of the meal, any sticky bits should have dropped off.

Hot! The sides of larger, metal-cased slow cookers may get hotter than you think. Always allow space around them and don't let children touch them.

Food safety. This is an important issue, so don't take risks.
· Never leave uncooked food in a slow cooker at room temperature for any length of time before starting cooking.
· Don't leave leftovers sitting around in the slow cooker bowl because they cool down very slowly. Refrigerate or freeze them as soon as possible.
· Avoid cooking meat or poultry before it has thawed completely or the thickest part may not be properly cooked.
· Consider buying a meat thermometer to ensure that the thickest part of the cut is cooked to the correct stage.

What features? If you are buying a slow cooker, check the features offered by the latest models. We like slow cookers with the basic functions of HIGH, LOW, OFF and KEEP WARM, but can manage pretty well with only HIGH and LOW. A dishwasher-safe bowl or insert is also a real bonus.

* The best feature we have come across lately is the rectangular metal (instead of ceramic) insert of the Breville BSC560. This has an excellent non-stick finish and can be used for browning on the stove top and/or in the oven for reheating if required.

Soups

Smoked Pork, Lentil and Vegetable Soup

A smoked pork hock from a butcher's shop weighs about 1kg and will give a very good, slightly smoky flavour to this really substantial soup. When the meat from the hock is completely tender, lift it out of the slow cooker, leave it on a tray to cool until it is easy to handle, then discard the bones etc. before cutting the meat into small cubes. We don't usually add the chopped pork skin, but you may like to add some of this to the soup too.

For about 8 servings:

1 smoked bacon hock, about 1kg

3½ litres (14 cups) hot water

1–2 cups chopped celery stalk (don't use leaves)

2 carrots, finely chopped

1 large onion, finely chopped

2–3 garlic cloves, optional

1 cup dried soup mix

½ cup pearl barley

½ cup red lentils

½–1 cup freshly chopped parsley

1. Turn a large slow cooker to HIGH.

2. Put the bacon hock in the slow cooker, add the hot water, then cover and let it start cooking while you prepare the vegetables.

3. Add the finely chopped vegetables to the slow cooker (but for the best flavour, first brown the chopped onion and garlic cloves in a frypan (or suitable slow cooker insert*), using a little oil until evenly and lightly browned).

4. Add the soup mix, barley and red lentils to the slow cooker. Cover and cook for about 10 hours on HIGH. You may like to stir the mixture part way through cooking to make sure that the dried grains, lentils, etc. do not stick to the bottom of the pot.

5. Lift out the hock when it is tender all the way through, then allow it to cool before chopping up the meat as described in the introduction to this recipe. Discard the bones.

6. Just before serving, stir in the chopped parsley.

7. Refrigerate or freeze any soup which is not eaten the day it is cooked.

NOTE: For extra flavour, tie a bunch of fresh herbs together with string and heat them in the soup for about 4–6 hours. Discard before serving.

* See the box on page 5.

HIGH for 4
hours or 8 hours
on LOW

For about 4 servings:

1 Tbsp canola or olive oil

1 medium–large onion, sliced

2cm piece root ginger, grated

2 cloves garlic, chopped

1 tsp curry powder

½ cup red lentils

1 kumara, about 400g,
peeled and cubed

3 cups boiling water

4 tsp chicken or vegetable
stock powder

1 x 400ml can coconut cream

Kumara, Coconut and Lentil Soup

This is one of Alison's favourite soups. You don't need to be fussy about the size (or colour) of the kumara – if you use a large kumara and find the soup is rather thick, just thin it with a little extra stock or water.

1 Put the oil and onion in a fairly large pot. Stir well and heat until the onion is lightly but evenly browned. Add the ginger, garlic and curry powder to the onion, and stir for 1–2 minutes.

2 Turn a medium-to-large slow cooker to HIGH or LOW, depending on how much time you have available, and tip in the onion mixture. Add the lentils, kumara, boiling water, stock powder and coconut cream.

3 Cook on HIGH for about 4 hours or on LOW for about 8 hours until the kumara is tender.

4 Purée the mixture in a food processor, then adjust the seasonings to taste. Serve immediately or reheat just before serving.

VARIATION: If you like a smooth soup, purée everything when the kumara is tender, then put it through a sieve.

This recipe is suitable for vegetarians if vegetable stock powder is used instead of chicken stock powder.

For 8 servings:

½ cup pearl barley

10 cups hot water

3 Tbsp stock powder (chicken stock, or your choice of flavours)

about 1 cup each finely chopped (or food processed) carrot and celery

1 large onion, finely chopped

2 tsp butter or canola oil

1 x 400g can chopped tomatoes in juice

lots of chopped parsley

"Comfort Food" Barley Broth

Barley broth was Alison's favourite winter soup when she was a child. Her mother would give her a mug of this soup when she arrived home from school in the late afternoon, and the world would instantly seem to be a better place. This recipe has since been handed on down through the family.

1 Coat the inside of the bowl of a medium-to-large slow cooker with non-stick spray, then add the barley, hot water and stock powder followed by the finely chopped carrot and celery.

2 Cook the onion in a frypan with the butter or oil until it is transparent and lightly browned, then add to the slow cooker. Add the tomatoes in juice, turn the cooker to LOW and forget about it for 10–12 hours.

3 Add the parsley just before serving.

NOTE: This soup can be turned on in the early evening, and turned off when you get up in the morning, then cooled and refrigerated until required. Or it can be refrigerated in the bowl of the slow cooker overnight, turned on when you get up in the morning, and enjoyed when you arrive home in the late afternoon.

It is not a good idea to leave room-temperature soup sitting around in a warm room for long in case bugs grow in it. Refrigerate the soup in smaller containers or in the slow cooker bowl if you have room for it in the fridge. You can also freeze containers of the soup for later use.

VARIATION: You can add other finely chopped vegetables or dried soup mix to this soup if you like, or cook a lamb shank in it. Please yourself – it is nice to make changes every now and then.

This recipe is suitable for vegetarians if vegetable stock powder is used instead of chicken stock powder.

HIGH for 4
hours or LOW
for 8–9 hours

Curried Red Lentil and Carrot Soup

We have a lot of time for little red lentils. They sit in jars in the pantry looking cheerful, year in and year out, providing good value for money. They also have a good flavour, as well as providing protein for vegetarians and meat-eaters. We hope you enjoy this soup as much as we do.

P.S. The lentils lighten in colour as they cook, so do not expect the soup to be bright red!

For 6 cups of creamy soup:

1 onion, finely sliced

2 cloves garlic, chopped

2 large or 4 smaller carrots, scrubbed and chopped

2 cups red lentils

8 cups boiling water

3 tsp vegetable (or other) stock powder

1 Tbsp butter

1 Tbsp curry powder

1. Coat the inside of the bowl of a medium-to-large slow cooker with non-stick spray and turn it to HIGH or LOW, depending on the cooking time that suits you.

2. Cut the onion into quarters, remove the skin, then slice finely. Add to the slow cooker with the garlic and carrot. Stir in the lentils, boiling water and stock powder.

3. Heat the butter and curry powder in a small pot until the mixture becomes aromatic, then tip it into the slow cooker. Spoon a little of the liquid from the slow cooker into the pot, swirl it round, then tip it back into the slow cooker.

4. Cover and cook on HIGH for 4 hours or LOW for 8–9 hours, then purée in a food processor or using a wand.

5. Pour the soup through a sieve and adjust seasonings if necessary according to taste.

6. Refrigerate the soup until it is required, up to 3–4 days. Heat individual bowls or mugs of soup in the microwave, or heat several servings at once in a pot on the stove, or in a slow cooker for about 2 hours on HIGH.

This recipe is suitable for vegetarians if vegetable stock powder is used instead of chicken stock powder.

For 6 servings (9 cups):

500g boneless, skinless
chicken thighs, cut into
1.5cm cubes

100g chorizo sausages,
thinly sliced

1 x 400g can chopped
tomatoes in juice

1 x 400g can creamed corn

2 stalks celery, thinly sliced

2 large cloves garlic,
finely chopped

1 red pepper, chopped,
optional

1 large onion, chopped

2 tsp Cajun seasoning

1½ tsp salt

¼ cup cornflour mixed with
½ cup cold water

4 cups chicken stock
(or 4 cups boiling water and
4 tsp chicken stock powder)

chopped parsley or chives to
garnish, optional

Spicy Cajun Chicken and Sausage Soup

This unusual and interesting soup is even more substantial when it is spooned over plain cooked rice. If you like spicy food, use a larger amount of Cajun seasoning (you'll find this in small jars in the spice section of the supermarket). Serve it for lunch or dinner, with a leafy green salad alongside if you like.

1. Coat the inside of the bowl of a medium-to-large slow cooker with non-stick spray and turn it to LOW. As you prepare each ingredient, put it in the slow cooker in the order given, then stir well. Cook for about 8 hours, stirring once or twice.

2. To serve, ladle cupfuls of the soup into bowls containing a generous amount of cooked rice. If you like, sprinkle with chopped parsley or chives. Refrigerate leftover soup, reheating in a microwave-proof dish when required.

TO COOK THE RICE: put 2 cups of long grain rice into a large, covered microwaveproof dish. Add 2 Tbsp canola oil, 1 tsp salt, and 4½ cups boiling water. Microwave on HIGH (100%) power for 25 minutes, then leave to stand for at least 5 minutes.

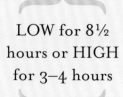

LOW for 8½ hours or HIGH for 3–4 hours

For 6 servings:

2 Tbsp canola oil

2 medium onions, quartered and sliced

2 cloves garlic, chopped

2–3cm piece root ginger, finely chopped

1 Tbsp curry powder

750g skinless boneless chicken thighs, diced

2 heaped Tbsp peanut butter

1 x 400ml can lite coconut cream

4 cups chicken stock (or 4 cups hot water plus 1 Tbsp instant chicken stock powder)

1 medium carrot, sliced

½ red pepper, deseeded and sliced

2 stalks lemongrass, halved

2–3 kaffir lime leaves

2 Tbsp light soy sauce

2 Tbsp brown sugar

1 Tbsp fish sauce

500g fresh egg noodles

2 cups green beans, fresh or frozen (thawed first)

chopped coriander leaves and/ or spring onion and/or a few beansprouts to garnish

Slow-cooked Chicken Laksa

We love laksa (creamy coconut-flavoured noodle soups). Although it is popular as a fast food option in the food courts found in New Zealand's larger cities, or from street vendors in parts of Asia, we think this slow cooker version works very well too. Don't be put off by the long list of ingredients as the method is really rather simple.

1 Heat the oil in a large pot (or suitable slow cooker insert*). Add the onion, garlic and ginger. Cook, stirring occasionally, until the onion has softened, then stir in the curry powder and cook for 1–2 minutes longer.

2 Add the diced chicken and stir-fry for a couple of minutes until it loses its pink colour. Transfer the chicken mixture to the slow cooker (or place the insert in the slow cooker). Stir in the peanut butter and coconut cream, then add the remaining ingredients except the noodles and the garnishes.

3 Cover, turn to LOW and cook for 6–8 hours or cook on HIGH for 3–4 hours. At the end of the cooking time, turn the slow cooker to HIGH, then add the noodles and beans and cook for 30 minutes.

4 Divide the noodles, vegetables and other goodies into bowls, then ladle in the soup. Scatter over the coriander and other garnishes and serve. Roti bread makes the perfect accompaniment.

* See the box on page 5.

Fish

For 4 lunch-sized servings:

2 Tbsp butter

1 cup basmati rice

4 cups boiling water

½ cup white wine

4 tsp chicken, vegetable or fish instant stock powder

4 spring onions

500g salmon steaks

Salmon Risotto

This rice and salmon dish makes an easy and delicious lunch or dinner. It is good at any time of the year, served with a salad in warm weather, or after soup during cooler months.

1. Turn the slow cooker to HIGH about 10 minutes before you start to assemble the ingredients.

2. Put the butter in the preheated slow cooker and tilt it so that the melted butter coats the base and sides. Stir in the basmati rice to coat the grains, then add the boiling water, white wine and stock powder.

3. Turn the cooker to LOW, cover, and leave the rice to cook for about 3½ hours.

4. After about 2 hours, chop the white and green parts of the spring onions and stir them into the partly cooked rice. However, if this is not possible, then add them just after the stock powder or close to the time when you are adding the salmon.

5. While the rice is cooking, cut the salmon steaks into pieces 2–3cm long, 1–2cm wide and about 7mm thick, removing and discarding any skin and bones. Refrigerate the prepared salmon until the rice is cooked, then stir it through the rice and spring onion mixture.

6. Cook on LOW for about 20 minutes or until a piece of salmon taken from the slow cooker separates when gently pulled apart with two forks. Serve on warmed plates.

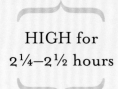

Easy Fish Pie

As the name suggests, this is an easily assembled mixture. You will get best results by using a large, shallow serving spoon or a saucer to serve individual portions. The idea of using a saucer may seem odd, but it really works well.

For 4 servings:

400g fish fillets (terakihi, monkfish or blue cod, etc.)

3 level Tbsp cornflour

1 x 400g can whole kernel corn, drained (reserve liquid)

1 cup frozen peas

200g cooked seafood such as prawns, scallops or shelled mussels, etc. (or extra fish)

1 cup liquid (make up with corn liquid, some milk and any liquid from mussels, etc.)

½–1 tsp salt

4 cups mashed potatoes

¼ cup grated cheese

¼ cup plain or golden breadcrumbs, optional

pinch of paprika, optional

1. Coat the inside of the bowl of a medium slow cooker with non-stick spray.

2. Cut the fish into 2–3cm cubes, removing any bones, then put them in the slow cooker. Sprinkle the cornflour over the fish and toss to mix evenly. Sprinkle the drained corn over the fish.

3. Microwave the frozen peas in a plastic bag (1–2 minutes at 100% power), then sprinkle them into the slow cooker.

4. Add the prawns, halved scallops, and halved mussels, etc. (or extra fish, instead).

5. Make the corn liquid up to 1 cup with milk and any liquid from the mussels, etc. and pour it evenly over the fish mixture. Add salt to taste.

6. Add the mashed potatoes in blobs, then use a fork or spoon to spread it out to cover everything, keeping the top rather rough.

7. Sprinkle the grated cheese – and the breadcrumbs and paprika if using – over the potato.

8. Turn the slow cooker to HIGH, cover and cook for 2¼–2½ hours.

9. Serve with individual bowls of salad greens.

NOTE: You may find golden breadcrumbs close to regular dried breadcrumbs in your supermarket. Golden breadcrumbs give a much more attractive colour to toppings or coatings and are well worth using.

For 4 servings:

Stock:

3 cups water

2 Tbsp wine vinegar

1 tsp salt

1 celery stalk

1 onion

1 carrot

1–2 cloves garlic

2 stalks parsley

500-600g salmon fillet, cut into 4 serving sized pieces

fresh dill sprigs to garnish, optional

Sauce:

¼ cup mayonnaise

¼ cup sour cream

2 Tbsp lemon juice

½ cup very finely chopped cucumber

2 Tbsp finely chopped fresh dill leaves

Simmered Salmon Slices with Creamy Sauce

When slices of salmon (cut crosswise from a side of salmon) are simmered gently in vegetable stock, they emerge very well flavoured and particularly tender. They can be served hot, warm or cold, with a creamy cucumber sauce. When served with new potatoes and a lettuce or watercress and tomato salad, you have a main course fit for a queen, without any last-minute hassles!

1. Make the stock first (you can make it ahead and refrigerate it or make it about an hour before you want to serve the meal).

2. Combine the water, vinegar and salt in a pot on the stove and bring to a simmer.

3. Roughly chop the vegetables and place into a food processor fitted with a chopping blade, then process until the vegetables are finely chopped.

4. Add the chopped vegetables to the pot and simmer for 20–30 minutes, then strain and discard the vegetables. Keep the stock at a low simmer until you are ready to transfer it to the slow cooker.

5. Turn the slow cooker to HIGH and leave to heat up for 15–30 minutes. While the slow cooker is heating, remove the salmon from the fridge and allow to come to room temperature.

6. Put the salmon slices in the slow cooker, add the hot stock, then cover and cook for 20–30 minutes or until the salmon is just cooked through. Discard the cooking liquid.

7. To make the sauce while the salmon is cooking, mix together the mayonnaise, sour cream, lemon juice, chopped cucumber and dill leaves.

8. Serve the salmon hot, warm, or at room temperature, with a spoonful of creamy sauce and a sprig of dill if desired.

Chicken

Soy Glazed Chicken Legs

The combination of soy and sweet chilli sauce gives chicken legs a mild but distinctive Asian flavour that should be a hit with the whole family.

For 4 servings:

2 Tbsp sweet chilli sauce

1 Tbsp sesame oil

¼ cup Kikkoman soy sauce

juice of ½ large or
1 small lemon

3 Tbsp brown sugar

4 whole chicken legs (thigh and drumstick)

2 Tbsp cornflour

2 Tbsp sherry (or water)

1. Coat the inside of the bowl of a medium slow cooker with non-stick spray and turn to HIGH.

2. Measure the first five ingredients into the slow cooker, then mix well with a non-stick stirrer.

3. Trim any extra fat off the chicken thigh, and turn each thigh in the sauce so all surfaces are coated. Have the outer sides (the side with more skin) of each leg on the bottom. Cover and cook on HIGH for 4 hours.

4. Mix together the cornflour and sherry and stir into the sauce to thicken.

5. Turn each leg in the sauce and serve with rice and a salad or cooked vegetables.

Herbed Boneless Whole Roast Chicken

While we were wandering round a local butcher's shop recently, we came across a netted boneless, stuffed chicken which we thought should cook well in a large, oval slow cooker. We were right! With the addition of fresh herbs from the garden and a sprinkling of paprika and turmeric etc., to stop the surface from looking pallid, we produced a colourful, flavourful, easy-to-slice chicken roll, which served five or six people, and tasted nearly as good cold the next day.

For 5–6 servings:

1 rolled boneless stuffed chicken, about 1kg

1 Tbsp canola or olive oil

4–6 large cloves garlic, cut into chunky slices

sprigs of fresh herbs, e.g. rosemary, sage or thyme

½ tsp each paprika, turmeric, mixed spice, cinnamon etc.

1. Remove the plastic covering from the chicken, then rinse briefly under a cold tap. Pat the chicken dry with paper towels, then drizzle oil over it, spreading it evenly with your hands.

2. Using a pointed knife, pierce the chicken in a number of places through the netting. Push a sliver of garlic into each cut, then push more slivers into the neck and tail ends, along with some herb sprigs.

3. Coat the inside of the bowl of an oval-shaped slow cooker with non-stick spray and turn to LOW. Scatter herb sprigs on the bottom of the cooker, then position the chicken in the cooker, breast-side down. Mix together the suggested spices, then sprinkle them through a fine sieve over the chicken as evenly as possible.

4. Cook on LOW for about 9 hours, then transfer the chicken to a cutting board. Using scissors, cut along the net and remove it, then cut the chicken into the desired number of slices (wrap any uncut roll with cling film, leave to cool, then refrigerate).

5. Strain the liquid from the slow cooker into a small microwave-proof jug or bowl. Heat until bubbling, then add enough cornflour and water paste to thicken it to use for chicken gravy. Taste, add salt if necessary, and serve.

NOTE: if you like, halve or quarter peeled kumara or potatoes, shake them in a plastic bag with a little oil, then push them down the sides of the chicken roll soon after you turn on the slow cooker. The vegetables look and taste good with a little of the seasoning mix on them too!

LOW for 8
hours or HIGH
for 2 hours,
then LOW for
4 hours

For 4–6 servings:

1 fresh or thawed chicken,
about 1.5kg

½ cup honey, preferably
amber honey

2 Tbsp butter

juice of half a lemon

1 tsp dried ginger or 2 tsp
freshly grated root ginger

1 tsp dark soy sauce

2 cloves garlic, grated or
finely chopped

Whole Chicken with Honey, Ginger and Garlic

The mixture that gives this chicken such a delicious flavour also makes it smell really good as it cooks. Turn on the slow cooker before you remove the chicken from your refrigerator or shopping basket, and assemble the other ingredients that you will need.

1. Coat the inside of the bowl of a medium slow cooker with non-stick spray and turn to LOW.

2. Discard any pieces of fat from the chicken's gut cavity. Run it under the cold tap, pat dry with a paper towel, then put the chicken, breast-side down, on a board. Firmly press down on it to reduce its height, then put it in the slow cooker. Cover.

3. Heat a pot or frypan, then add to it the honey, butter, lemon juice, ginger, soy sauce, and the garlic. Stir together until it is well mixed.

4. Using a pastry brush, generously brush some of the honey mixture over the chicken, then cover again.

5. As the chicken cooks, baste it about 4 times with more of the mixture. The exact timing for the basting is not important.

6. About halfway through the cooking time, turn the chicken over so it is breast-side up and baste.

7. The chicken is cooked when a skewer inserted into the thick part of a thigh shows no pink juice. Turn off the slow cooker and leave the chicken to stand until you are ready to carve and serve it.

8. Spoon some of the juices over each serving. (If you like, you can reheat and thicken the pan juices and any of the leftover basting mixture in the pan, with a little more cornflour paste. This makes a delicious sauce.)

Chicken, Kumara and Cranberry Stew

This easily put-together stew is particularly good in autumn and winter, but we also enjoy it at other times of year.

For 4–6 servings:

1kg boneless chicken thighs

½–¾ cup dried cranberries

1 medium onion, finely chopped

2 tsp grated root ginger

1 Tbsp honey

1 Tbsp wine or cider vinegar

1 tsp salt

1 Tbsp cornflour or arrowroot

1 cup liquid chicken stock or 2 tsp instant chicken stock powder dissolved in 1 cup warm water

500g orange-fleshed kumara, cut in 2–3cm chunks

2 sprigs parsley, chopped

1. Coat the inside of the bowl of a large slow cooker with non-stick spray and turn to HIGH.

2. Cut each boneless thigh into three or four pieces lengthwise, then put them in the slow cooker. Add the cranberries and the finely chopped onion.

3. Mix together in a microwave-proof bowl all the remaining ingredients except the kumara and parsley. Stir until no lumps remain, warming everything in the bowl (try about 30 seconds at 100% power) if necessary to melt the honey, etc.

4. Pour the mixture into the slow cooker, cover and cook on HIGH for 2 hours.

5. Add the kumara and cook for 2–2½ hours longer until the chicken and the kumara are tender.

6. Sprinkle with chopped parsley before serving. Pan-cooked cabbage or simmered silverbeet go well with this stew.

VARIATION: Make a bouquet garni by tying together sprigs of thyme, sage, oreganum, etc. and put this in the slow cooker. Remove it before serving the mixture.

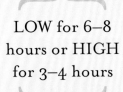

LOW for 6–8
hours or HIGH
for 3–4 hours

For 2 servings:

¼ cup dry sherry

¼ cup Kikkoman soy sauce

2 Tbsp brown sugar

4–5 bone-in skinless chicken thighs

2 Tbsp flour

1 tsp cornflour

Chicken Teriyaki

Our families and friends love the well-flavoured sauce in which this chicken is cooked. For a change we sometimes add pineapple pieces – they make an interesting addition, but they are certainly not a necessity.

1 Coat the inside of the bowl of a medium slow cooker with non-stick spray and turn to HIGH or LOW, depending on time available.

2 Measure the sherry, soy sauce and brown sugar into the cooker and mix with a plastic stirrer until the sugar is dissolved.

3 Pat the chicken thighs dry with a paper towel, then sieve the flour over them until evenly coated.

4 Transfer the floured thighs to the slow cooker one at a time and turn to coat with the sauce. Cover and cook on LOW for 6–8 hours or HIGH for 3–4 hours.

VARIATION: Add halved pineapple rings to the slow cooker about an hour before the chicken will be ready.

Just before serving, mix the cornflour with a little water or pineapple syrup, pile up the chicken in one end of the slow cooker, and stir in the cornflour mixture to thicken the sauce. Turn each chicken thigh in the sauce before serving, and spoon any remaining sauce over. Serve with rice and brightly coloured seasonal vegetables.

HIGH for
2½–3 hours

Kirsten's Chicken Thighs with Beans

Kirsten, Alison's daughter, enjoyed a baked chicken when eating out in a restaurant in Napier. A few days later she decided to try a slow cooker version at home. We all liked it, and hope that you will too – it is a really easy recipe once you have assembled the ingredients.

For 2 large or 4 smallish servings:

1 onion, finely diced

1 red pepper, deseeded and finely diced

1 yellow pepper, deseeded and finely diced

150g bacon, cut in strips crosswise

4 skinless, boneless chicken thighs (500–600g in total)

1 x 440g can cannellini beans

arrowroot, potato starch or cornflour to thicken

chopped parsley, thyme and sage (or other fresh herbs)

1. Coat the inside of the bowl of a medium slow cooker with non-stick spray.

2. Put the prepared onion, peppers and bacon in the slow cooker and turn to HIGH.

3. Bang the chicken thighs with a meat hammer to flatten them. Put the flattened thighs, skin-side up, on top of the vegetables in the slow cooker. (If you need to make 2 layers of chicken, put half the vegetable and bacon mixture between the layers of chicken.)

4. Pour the beans and their liquid over the chicken, then cover and cook on HIGH for 2½–3 hours.

5. Mix 1 tablespoon of arrowroot (or whichever starch you are using) with 2–3 tablespoons of water and stir it into the liquid to thicken. Repeat with more starch and water until the liquid has thickened.

6. Sprinkle with chopped herbs just before serving. Serve with pan-cooked cabbage or silverbeet or a green side salad.

VARIATION: For extra flavour brown the chopped onion in a little oil before mixing it with the chopped peppers.

LOW for 6–7
hours, then
HIGH for 1 hour

For 8 servings:

¼ cup blanched almonds

2 Tbsp sesame seeds

2 Tbsp canola oil

1 medium-large onion, diced

2–3 cloves garlic, chopped

1 tsp ground cumin

1 tsp chilli powder (use chipotle [smoked chilli] powder if available)

½ tsp cinnamon

¼ cup cocoa powder

2 Tbsp tomato paste

2 x 400g cans diced tomatoes in juice

1.5–2kg chicken pieces (drumsticks, thighs, whole legs, etc.)

1 tsp salt

Chicken Mole

Chicken mole is a traditional Mexican dish – the original recipe is renowned for its long list of ingredients and lengthy preparation. We've stripped the ingredients back and streamlined the preparation, so you can let your slow cooker do the work and you just have to sit back and enjoy the delicious results.

1. Combine the almonds and sesame seeds in a blender or food processor and process until finely chopped.

2. Heat the oil in a large frypan (or suitable slow cooker insert*), then add the diced onion and chopped garlic. Cook, stirring frequently until the onion is soft, then add the ground nut mixture, cumin, chilli powder and cinnamon and stir-fry for about 1 minute. Sprinkle in the cocoa powder, then stir in the tomato paste and diced tomatoes and juice.

3. Coat the inside of the bowl of a medium-to-large slow cooker with non-stick spray (or place the insert in the cooker). Add the chicken pieces, then stir in the sauce to coat the chicken. Cover and cook on LOW for 6–7 hours or until the chicken is very tender.

4. Remove the bones from the chicken meat and discard them (the meat should be tender enough to fall off the bones). Set the lid ajar or remove it completely and turn to HIGH for 1 hour to thicken the sauce. Season to taste with the salt.

5. Serve spooned over rice or use as a filling for soft tortillas.

✱ See the box on page 5.

Mince
& Sausages

LOW for 8 hours or HIGH for 4 hours

Sweet and Sour Meat Patties

Good old mince! It's always great value for money and as popular with children as it is with adults. The easy sweet and sour sauce that goes with this dish calls only for long-lasting store-cupboard ingredients.

For 4 servings:

500g minced beef

½ cup milk

½ cup dry breadcrumbs

2 tsp garlic salt or 1 tsp salt

1 tsp dried oregano

Sauce:

1 Tbsp cider vinegar or wine vinegar

2 Tbsp tomato sauce

2 Tbsp sweet chilli sauce

2 Tbsp brown sugar

1. Measure the first five ingredients into a bowl and mix well. Or you can combine the ingredients in a plastic bag and use your hand (outside the bag) to 'squish' everything together. Divide the mixture in half, then into quarters, then into eighths. Using wet hands, roll each piece into a ball, then flatten to about 2–3cm thick.

2. Heat a little oil in a large frypan (or suitable slow cooker insert*), then brown the patties, a few at a time. While the patties are browning, coat the inside of the bowl of a medium slow cooker with non-stick spray. Transfer the browned patties into the slow cooker and turn to LOW (or place the insert in the slow cooker).

3. Mix the sauce ingredients in the unwashed frypan or a small bowl, then pour it over the patties in the slow cooker. Cover and cook for 8 hours on LOW or for 4 hours on HIGH.

4. Serve the patties and sauce with vegetables such as mashed potatoes, broccoli or green beans, and carrots.

✳ See the box on page 5.

For 4 servings:

1 medium onion,
roughly chopped

2 carrots, chopped

1 cup sliced celery stalks

1 large or 2 small (about
500g in total) kumara, sliced
lengthwise then chopped
crosswise

1 tsp oregano

1 x 400g can chopped
tomatoes in juice

¼ cup water

1 tsp salt

Meatballs:

1 medium onion, roughly
chopped

2 cloves garlic, roughly
chopped

1 tsp dried oregano

1 egg

1 tsp salt

500g minced beef

½ cup dried breadcrumbs

Meatballs and Vegetables in Gravy

This is an easy one-dish recipe in which you simply put some roughly chopped vegetables, a can of tomatoes and some seasonings in the slow cooker and while they heat through, you make meatballs using the food processor. Then all you have to do is brown them, add them to the slow cooker, and forget about dinner until it's serving time!

1. Coat the inside of the bowl of a medium slow cooker with non-stick spray and turn to LOW. Add the first three ingredients to the slow cooker.

2. Peel and slice the kumara lengthwise, then cut them crosswise into chunky pieces. Add to the slow cooker. Sprinkle the oregano over the vegetables, then pour in the canned tomatoes and juice. Add the water, sprinkle on the salt, then cover and start thinking about the meatballs.

3. Using a food processor, finely chop the roughly cut onion and the garlic. Add the oregano, egg and salt, then briefly process again. Break up the mince into half a dozen small chunks and add to the processor, one at a time and briefly process. Sprinkle in the breadcrumbs, then pulse in bursts just until the crumbs are mixed evenly through.

4. Tip the mince mixture onto the bench and cut into quarters, then cut each quarter into four smaller chunks to make 16 altogether. Using wet hands, roll each chunk into a ball. Brown the balls, 8 at a time, in a frypan with a drizzle of oil, shaking the pan frequently. Tip the browned meatballs into the slow cooker and cook for 7½–8 hours.

5. Serve drizzled with a little sweet chilli sauce.

For 4 servings:

1 Tbsp canola or olive oil

1 large red or brown onion, chopped

2 cloves garlic, chopped

500g minced beef

1 x 37g packet cream of chicken soup

1 x 420g can baked beans

1 x 400g can chopped tomatoes in juice

1 tsp hot sauce, optional

2 tsp Worcestershire sauce

Easy Mince and Bean Bake

Here's an easy meal for a busy day! Make it after lunch and cook it on HIGH for 4 hours, or get a head start and assemble everything the night before, in which case you'll need to refrigerate it overnight, or assemble it after breakfast, and cook it on LOW all day. The cooked mixture is good served on rice or spaghetti, or in bowls with a salad alongside.

1. Heat the oil in a large frypan (or suitable slow cooker insert*), then add the chopped onion and garlic. Cook until golden brown, stirring frequently. Add the mince to the pan in chunks, breaking them up as they brown.

2. Coat the inside of the bowl of a medium slow cooker with non-stick spray, then tip in the browned mixture (or place the insert in the slow cooker). Add the remaining ingredients and mix well to break up any lumps of soup mix.

3. Cover and cook on HIGH for 4 hours or LOW for 8 hours.

   NOTE: If you are really short of time, don't brown the mixture first – just put everything in together. It won't have such a good flavour, but it'll save time. A dash of dark soy sauce will improve its colour.

✳ See the box on page 5.

For about 8 servings:

canola or other oil

2 large onions, chopped

600g minced beef

2 tsp instant beef powder

2 x 420g cans Salsa Chilli Beans (medium heat)

Topping:

1 onion, finely chopped

50g butter, soft, but not melted

1 x 400g can whole kernel corn, plus liquid

1 cup cornmeal (instant polenta)

1 cup self-raising flour

1 cup grated tasty cheese

1 cup milk

¼ tsp paprika

Kirsten's Cornbread-topped Chilli Beans

This is a great recipe to make in a fairly large slow cooker to serve to a bunch of friends as it feeds about eight people. When there are four of us, we eat the first half and then refrigerate or freeze the other half to enjoy later. The flavour of the reheated mixture is just as good, if not even better, as the first lot! It's not too hot and spicy – fine for teenagers as well as adults, but it may be a bit too spicy for young children. We enjoy it in summer or winter, served with a crisp green salad and cold beer!

1 Coat the inside of the bowl of a large slow cooker with non-stick spray and turn it to HIGH.

2 Heat a little canola oil in a large frypan and brown the onion over a fairly high heat. Tip the browned onion into the slow cooker.

3 Add a little extra oil to the frypan, then stir in the mince, broken into small chunks. Raise the heat so that the mince browns quite quickly, breaking it up as it cooks. Transfer the cooked mince to the slow cooker. Sprinkle the beef stock over the mince, then pour in the contents of both cans of beans. Mix well.

4 To make the topping, combine all the ingredients except the paprika in a bowl in the order given. Stir to mix well. Pour the mixture evenly over the mince mixture, sprinkle with just a little paprika for extra colour, then cover and cook on LOW for 8 hours or HIGH for 4 hours.

For 4 servings:

2 Tbsp olive or canola oil

1 medium onion, diced

1 medium carrot, diced

2 sticks celery, diced

2 cloves garlic, chopped

500g beef mince

½ cup tomato paste

¼ cup brown sugar

¼ cup Worcestershire sauce

2 Tbsp wine vinegar

1 tsp dried oregano

1 tsp smoked paprika

salt and pepper to taste

To serve:

hamburger buns or bread rolls

coleslaw

sliced gherkins or pickles

potato crisps

Sloppy Joes

Sloppy Joes, made from mince cooked in a slightly smoky barbecue sauce and served in a bun with extras, are a tasty and easy alternative way of serving this perennial family favourite meat.

1. Heat the oil in a large frypan (or suitable metal slow cooker insert*) and sauté the prepared vegetables until they begin to soften.

2. Transfer the softened vegetables to the non-stick sprayed slow cooker (or place the insert in the slow cooker), then add the remaining ingredients except the salt and pepper and stir to combine.

3. Set the slow cooker to HIGH and cook for 4 hours (or cook on LOW for 8 hours). If possible, check once or twice during the later stages of cooking and add about ¼ cup of hot water at a time if the mixture looks dry – it shouldn't be runny, but should just hold its shape.

4. Season to taste with salt and pepper, then serve on split hamburger buns or bread rolls (toast or brown, if desired). A spoonful of coleslaw and a slice of pickle on top and some potato crisps on the side make for a delicious meal.

✳ See the box on page 5.

For 4 servings:

1 large or 2 smaller onions

1 Tbsp canola or other oil

500g sausages

1 x 410g can diced peaches
in syrup

1 Tbsp Kikkoman soy sauce

Savoury Sausages with Peaches

For best results, brown the sliced onions and the whole sausages before cooking them in the slow cooker, (or cook them in a slow cooker with a metal insert*). However, if you don't feel up to doing this, just put them in without browning them first – it won't be the end of the world!

Do make the effort, however, just before serving, to remove the cooked sausages, one or two at a time, and slice each one diagonally into five or six pieces. Once they're sliced, stir the pieces into the sauce. The mixture will look better and be easier for children to eat.

1 Coat the inside of the bowl of a medium slow cooker with non-stick spray.

2 Halve, then quarter the onion(s) from top to bottom, remove the skin and slice crosswise from top to bottom. Heat the oil in a large frypan and cook the onion until it is lightly browned, then transfer it to the slow cooker.

3 Brown the sausages in the same pan, adding a little extra oil only if really necessary.

4 While the sausages brown, open the can of peaches and add to the slow cooker with ¼ cup of the peach syrup and the soy sauce, reserving the remaining syrup. Turn the slow cooker to LOW, cover and cook for 8 hours (or HIGH for 4 hours).

5 At the end of the cooking time, remove the sausages from the slow cooker and cut each one diagonally into five or six slices. Return them to the slow cooker and stir. If the mixture looks dryish, add some or all of the reserved peach syrup.

6 Serve the sausage mixture with plenty of mashed potatoes and with green beans, peas, or pan-cooked cabbage.

For 4 servings:

500g pork sausages

1–2 Tbsp canola oil

1 large onion, chopped

1 cup (225g) basmati rice

8 dried apricots

2–3 stalks celery, chopped

3 tsp instant chicken stock powder and 1 tsp garlic-flavoured stock powder

3 cups hot water

¼ cup chopped parsley

Sausage Pilaf

It's worth taking a few minutes to brown the sausages and onions for this recipe as it improves their colour and flavour. Don't be tempted to leave out the dried apricot – it's there because it gives the pilaf an interesting taste.

1. Coat the inside of the bowl of a medium slow cooker with non-stick spray.

2. Brown the sausages in a fairly large frypan in a drizzle of oil, then transfer them to the slow cooker.

3. Brown the chopped onion in 1 tablespoon of oil, then add the rice. Cook for a few minutes longer, then transfer the contents of the pan into the slow cooker.

4. Using kitchen scissors, chop the dried apricots directly into the slow cooker, then stir in the chopped celery.

5. Combine the chicken and garlic stock powders in a measuring jug, then stir in the hot water. Mix well and pour into the slow cooker to cover the sausages.

6. Cover and cook on LOW for 5–5½ hours or until the rice is tender and most of the liquid has been absorbed. Sprinkle with the chopped parsley and serve in shallow bowls.

VARIATION: Lift out one or two cooked sausages at a time and cut each into four or five diagonal slices. Return the slices to the slow cooker and mix well.

LOW for
7–8 hours

For 4 servings:

2 Tbsp olive oil

1 medium onion, diced

2 sticks celery, diced

1 medium carrot, grated

2 cloves garlic, chopped

1 tsp dried basil

½ tsp dried oregano

½ tsp salt

2 x 400g cans diced
tomatoes in juice

2 Tbsp tomato paste

500–600g Italian-style
sausages

Sausage Meatballs and Tomato Sauce

Simon's kids love spaghetti and meatballs, but sometimes shaping meatballs can be a bit of a pain. He started wondering if there might be an easier way. What would happen, he asked himself, if you just cut sausages into shorter lengths and added them to a sauce? We're very pleased with the results, plus it is definitely quicker and easier than making conventional meatballs. Although our recipe calls for Italian-style sausages, you can use any kind of sausages.

1. Heat the oil in a large frypan (or suitable slow cooker insert*), then add the onion, celery, carrot and garlic. Cook, stirring occasionally, until the vegetables have softened.

2. Coat the inside of the bowl of a medium slow cooker with non-stick spray. Transfer the softened vegetables to the slow cooker (or put the insert into the slow cooker). Add the herbs, salt, tomatoes and juice and the tomato paste and stir to combine.

3. Cut the sausages into 2–3cm long pieces and gently stir into the sauce in the slow cooker. Cover, turn to LOW and cook for 7–8 hours.

4. Adjust the seasonings to taste, then serve over cooked spaghetti.

✷ See the box on page 5.

Beef & Lamb

Spicy Shin Beef and Vegetable Casserole

Beef from the shin is lean, with connective tissue between the muscle. Long, slow cooking turns both the meat and the connective tissue into very tender, well-flavoured meat – definitely one of our favourites! Buy the meat on the bone, as we did when we made this recipe, or buy cubed shin beef meat. Please yourself!

For 4–6 servings:

800g shin beef on the bone (500–600g if boneless)

2 onions, chopped

2 tsp canola oil

2 tsp curry powder

1 Tbsp brown sugar

1 tsp salt

1 Tbsp Worcestershire sauce

2 medium potatoes, halved

2 medium carrots, scrubbed and cut into 1cm pieces

2 cups water

1 Tbsp cornflour mixed with 2–3 Tbsp cold water

1 cup frozen peas

1. Coat the inside of the bowl of a medium-to-large slow cooker with non-stick spray and turn to HIGH.

2. Put the pieces of shin beef in the cooker.

3. In a frypan cook the onion in the oil over medium heat until golden brown. While the onion is cooking, sprinkle the curry powder, brown sugar, salt and Worcestershire sauce over the meat in the slow cooker.

4. Add the prepared potatoes and carrots to the slow cooker, sprinkle in the sautéed onions, then pour in the water.

5. After 7 hours, lift out the beef and remove and discard the bones. Cut the beef into smaller pieces if you like, then return it to the slow cooker. Mix together the cornflour and cold water and stir into the cooking liquid. Add the frozen peas and cook for 30 minutes longer.

6. Check the seasoning and adjust to taste, then serve in shallow bowls. Refrigerate leftovers in a covered container for later use.

For 3–4 servings:

1kg beef spare ribs, cut 1–1.5cm thick

½ cup tomato sauce

2 Tbsp Worcestershire sauce

¼ cup water

¼ cup maple syrup or 2 rounded Tbsp golden syrup

2–3 garlic cloves, finely chopped

Glazed Beef Spare Ribs

To make these delicious browned ribs, look, or ask for them in a butcher's shop (you may have to order them). You may think that 1kg is a large amount for three or four people, but there is a high proportion of bone to meat!

1. Coat the inside of the bowl of a medium-to-large slow cooker with non-stick spray and turn it to HIGH or LOW, depending on the cooking time that suits you.

2. If the spare ribs are in long pieces, cut each strip in half crosswise. In a large, heavy frypan, brown a few of the spare ribs at a time over high heat, then transfer them to the slow cooker, discarding the fat.

3. Stir together the remaining ingredients, then drizzle the mixture over the spare ribs. Cover and cook on HIGH for 6–8 hours or LOW for 8–12 hours until the meat is very tender.

4. These ribs are good served on plainly cooked rice. Spoon the remaining sauce over the meat and rice, and serve with a mixed salad alongside. (Have a bowl handy for nibbled bones!)

Oriental Beef with Hokkien Noodles

This is an easy, delicious meal with an interesting flavour that may be too strong for young children. We serve half the cooked mixture for two adults, and refrigerate the other half in a covered container, then microwave and eat it a couple of days later. Dark soy sauce, sesame oil and hot chilli sauce are available at stores selling Chinese ingredients (they will keep for years, but you may well find that you can add the soy and hot chilli sauces to everyday stews and casseroles for extra colour and flavour). You'll find precooked, vacuum-packed Chinese Hokkien noodles near the pasta section in your supermarket.

For 4 servings:

about 600g skirt steak

2 Tbsp canola oil

2 large onions, sliced

250g button mushrooms, quartered

¼ cup dark soy sauce

¼ cup sherry

1 Tbsp sesame oil

1–2cm piece root ginger, grated

1 star anise

1 tsp hot chilli sauce

2 x 400g packs Hokkien noodles

1. Lightly flour the skirt steak and brown both sides in a heavy frypan in a little of the oil. Set aside the browned steak and add more oil to the pan, then lightly brown the onion and the mushrooms.

2. Coat the inside of the bowl of a medium-to-large slow cooker with non-stick spray. Cut the browned steak into diagonal strips across the grain of the meat, then again into shorter lengths and put them in the slow cooker. Stir through the browned onion and mushroom mixture, then the remaining ingredients except for the noodles.

3. Cover and cook on LOW for 7 hours, then stir through the noodles. (If you cut one side from the noodle pack, then run some warm water into it you will find that the noodles become flexible and easy to remove. Be sure to drain off the water from the pack.) After adding the noodles, cook for about 1 hour longer.

4. If necessary, thicken the sauce with a little cornflour or arrowroot and water paste before serving.

NOTE: To add some colour, cut a smallish head of broccoli into bite-sized florets and a red or orange pepper into short strips. Stir-fry the vegetables in a little oil and 1 teaspoon of water for about 5 minutes, then drain and stir through the beef and noodles just before serving.

For 6–8 servings:

about 2kg ox cheeks

¼ cup plain flour

oil

4 cloves garlic, chopped

¼ cup tomato paste

½ cup tomato sauce

1½ cups fresh or flat beer or stout

4 tsp dark soy sauce

2–3 bay leaves, optional

Ox Cheek and Beer Casserole

Ox cheek is one of Alison's favourite foods. You'll need to order it from your friendly butcher or from the man behind the meat counter in your supermarket as it's not usually on display. To buy a kilogram (equivalent to two cheeks) will cost you about $7. Since you shouldn't need to trim anything from the meat, it is good value for money!

1. Cut each ox cheek into several slices and place on a sheet of baking paper. Sprinkle the meat with the flour, turning the pieces so they are evenly coated.

2. Brown the floured slices on both sides in a large frypan containing just enough oil to coat the bottom of the pan.

3. While the meat browns, coat the inside of the bowl of a large slow cooker with non-stick spray. Cut the browned meat into bite-size pieces and put in the slow cooker.

4. Add the remaining ingredients to the cooker and stir to mix. Cover and cook for 6–7 hours on HIGH.

5. If the gravy seems thin when the meat is cooked, stir in a little cornflour and water mixed together to make a paste.

6. Serve with mashed potatoes and colourful vegetables, or on rice, with a salad alongside.

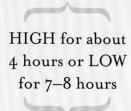

HIGH for about 4 hours or LOW for 7–8 hours

For 4–5 servings:

500g minced beef

1 large red or white onion, finely chopped

2 cloves garlic, finely chopped

1 x 37g packet cream of chicken soup

1 x 400g can chopped tomatoes in thick juice

1 x 425g can baked beans

2 tsp Worcestershire sauce, optional

Easy Beef and Bean Bake

This easy recipe is especially popular with teenagers. Serve it on spaghetti, or on rice, or spoon it into bowls – whichever your family likes best. Almost everything except the mince can come from your store cupboard. Remember to replace these staples promptly so you can make the recipe again soon.

1. Brown the minced beef in a frypan over medium heat. Add the chopped onion and garlic to the mince, then turn up the heat. Stir occasionally until everything is lightly browned.

2. Meanwhile, coat the inside of the bowl of a medium-to-large slow cooker with non-stick spray, then add the soup, tomatoes, baked beans and Worcestershire sauce. Add the mince and onion mixture to the slow cooker and mix well. Cover and cook on HIGH for about 4 hours or LOW for 7–8 hours.

3. Serve on freshly cooked rice or spaghetti, or spoon the mixture into shallow bowls. Sprinkle with a little grated cheese or some chopped parsley if desired.

4. Refrigerate leftovers, reheating them in the microwave oven when desired.

LOW
for 8 hours

Gingery Corned Beef

One of the ways we add extra flavour to corned beef is to simmer it in ginger ale. The other day, as Alison was unwrapping a lovely-looking piece of corned silverside, a knob of root ginger on the bench beside it caught her eye. No sooner thought of but done – grated ginger went into the cooking water along with a few other flavourings and the result was delicious. We hope that you like it too.

For about 8 servings:

1.5–2kg corned silverside

2 litres hot water

3–4cm piece root ginger

3 large cloves garlic

1½ tsp salt

sprigs of fresh rosemary and sage or 1 tsp dried mixed herbs

1 Coat the inside of the bowl of a medium-to-large slow cooker with non-stick spray and turn it to LOW. Put the meat and the hot water into the slow cooker.

2 Grate the ginger into the cooker, then chop and add the garlic. Sprinkle in the salt and herb sprigs or dried herbs. Cover and cook for 8 hours.

NOTE: To make a sauce to go with the corned beef, melt 2 Tbsp of butter in a pot. Stir in 2 Tbsp of flour and stir until it bubbles, then gradually add about 1 cup of strained cooking liquid, a little at a time, stirring constantly. Add a little cream and 1–2 tsp of dried mustard if desired. Spoon a little sauce over each serving of beef.

HINT: It is useful to have a piece of root ginger on hand. Put it in a bowl with garlic, etc. where it will keep for 2–3 weeks, or refrigerate or freeze it. You can grate it with a sharp grater, even when it is frozen. You'll be surprised by the way it adds flavour to different foods.

LOW
for 6–8 hours

For 4 servings:

3 slices bread, crumbed

6 sun-dried tomato halves, chopped

1–2 Tbsp chopped fresh basil leaves or 1 tsp dried

2–3 slices prosciutto, chopped, optional

½ tsp salt

black pepper to taste

750g beef schnitzel

toothpicks to fasten

2 Tbsp canola or other vegetable oil

1 medium onion, diced

2 cloves garlic, chopped

1 Tbsp plain flour

1 x 400g can diced tomatoes in juice

1 Tbsp balsamic vinegar

salt and pepper

Beef Olives in Tomato Sauce

Beef olives might have slipped out of foodie fashion these days, but we think it's possible they'll be making a comeback! Very lean beef schnitzel can sometimes be a bit tough, but long slow cooking makes it melt-in-the-mouth tender.

1 Make the filling by combining the first six ingredients in a large bowl.

2 Working with one at a time, lay the schnitzels on a board, then cut each into two halves long or wide enough to be rolled up. Place about ¼ cup of the filling mixture at one end of each schnitzel strip, then roll it up around the filling and secure with a toothpick.

3 Heat 1 tablespoon of the oil in a large frypan and brown the rolled schnitzels on all sides.

4 Coat the inside of the bowl of a medium-to-large slow cooker with non-stick spray. Transfer the browned schnitzels to the slow cooker or set aside until required.

5 Add the rest of the oil to the frypan, then sprinkle in the onion and garlic. Cook, stirring frequently, until the onion has softened, then stir in the flour. Cook for 1 minute further, then add the tomatoes and juice, vinegar and salt and pepper to taste. Bring the mixture to the boil, then pour it over the beef olives in the slow cooker and cover.

6 Turn the slow cooker to LOW and cook for 6–8 hours.

LOW
for 8–10 hours

For 6–8 servings:

1 cup desiccated coconut

Spice paste:

1 red onion, roughly chopped

3 cloves garlic

2–3cm piece root ginger

2 Tbsp fish sauce

2 Tbsp paprika

2 tsp ground cumin

2 tsp ground coriander

1 tsp (or more to taste) chilli powder

2 Tbsp oil

1 x 400ml coconut cream, regular or lite

1–1.2kg gravy beef, cut into 3cm cubes

2 Tbsp brown sugar

1 Tbsp tamarind paste or 2 Tbsp lemon juice

1 cinnamon stick

2–3 kaffir lime leaves, thinly sliced

½–1 tsp salt

Beef Rendang

The list of ingredients for this delicious curry is rather long, but the method is very simple. In fact, most of the ingredients are just blended together to make the spice paste.

1 Heat the coconut in a large dry pot or frypan (or suitable slow cooker insert*), stirring frequently until it is a uniform golden brown. Remove from the pan and set aside.

2 Combine the eight spice paste ingredients in a blender or food processor. Blend or process until it forms a smooth-looking paste.

3 Heat the oil in the pan (or suitable slow cooker insert). Add the spice paste and cook for about 5 minutes, stirring constantly. Stir in the coconut cream.

4 Coat the inside of the bowl of a large slow cooker with non-stick spray. Pour the sauce into the slow cooker (or place the insert into the slow cooker), then add the remaining ingredients, except the salt, and the toasted coconut. Stir to combine.

5 Cover, then turn to LOW and cook for 8–10 hours.

6 Season to taste with the salt and remove the cinnamon stick, then serve over steamed rice. A cucumber or green salad and roti or naan bread make ideal accompaniments.

✳ See the box on page 5.

For 4–6 servings:

¼ cup fine ground espresso coffee

1 Tbsp sugar

1 tsp smoked paprika

1 tsp garlic salt

½ tsp each ground cumin, coriander and black pepper

1–1.5kg beef rump

2 Tbsp olive or canola oil

1 medium onion, diced

1 Tbsp plain flour

1 cup strong coffee

½ cup tomato sauce

¼ cup brown sugar

¼ cup Worcestershire sauce

2 Tbsp balsamic vinegar

Coffee Braised Beef Rump

Coffee may sound like an unusual ingredient to include with meat, but in fact it really just adds a slight smokiness and an extra depth of flavour to the barbecue-style sauce. Don't be put off if you're not a big coffee fan; you'll never even know it's there.

1. Mix together 2 tablespoons of the ground coffee with the sugar, paprika, garlic salt and spices in a small bowl, then rub the mixture over the beef. Wrap in cling film, then leave to stand for at least 1 hour (or overnight).

2. Heat half the oil in a large frypan (or suitable slow cooker insert*) over a medium-high heat. Add the spice-coated beef and brown it well on all sides (about 3 minutes per side). Remove the beef and set aside.

3. Add the remaining oil to the pan (or slow cooker insert), then cook the diced onion for about 5 minutes, stirring occasionally, until the onion is soft. Stir in the flour and cook for about 1 minute longer, then add the remaining ingredients and stir to combine.

4. Coat the inside of the bowl of a medium-to-large slow cooker with non-stick spray. Place the beef in the slow cooker, then pour in the sauce (or place the insert into the slow cooker, then add the browned beef).

5. Cover, then turn to LOW and cook for 8–10 hours. About half an hour or an hour before you want to serve, remove the beef from the slow cooker and set it aside (covering it with foil to keep it warm). Turn the slow cooker to HIGH and leave the sauce to simmer, uncovered, for 30 minutes to thicken. If desired, stir in 1–2 teaspoons of cornflour mixed to a paste with 1–2 tablespoons of cold water.

6. Carefully slice the beef and arrange on a serving platter or plates and pour the thickened sauce over. Alternatively, add the sliced beef back to the sauce in the slow cooker.

7. Serve with mashed potatoes and lightly cooked vegetables or coleslaw for a delicious meal.

✳ See the box on page 5.

LOW for
6–8 hours

Greek-style Lamb with Orzo and Spinach

This dish is delicious and incredibly simple – a great combination. The orzo isn't actually cooked in the slow cooker, but the whole process is still so simple, we're sure you won't hold it against us!

For 3–4 servings:

500–600g diced lamb

2 cloves garlic, chopped

1 tsp dried oregano

1 tsp paprika

zest of ½ lemon

juice of 1 lemon

½ tsp salt

2 Tbsp olive oil

250g orzo

salt and pepper to taste

250g baby spinach leaves

50–100g feta cheese, crumbled

1. Coat the inside of the bowl of a medium-sized slow cooker with non-stick spray. Put the diced lamb in the slow cooker and sprinkle with the chopped garlic, oregano, paprika, lemon zest, half of the lemon juice and half of the olive oil. Stir to combine. Turn the slow cooker to LOW, then cover and cook for 6–8 hours.

2. About half an hour before you want to serve the meal, cook the orzo according to the packet instructions. Drain the cooked pasta thoroughly, then stir it into the mixture in the slow cooker along with the remaining olive oil and lemon juice. Season to taste with salt and pepper, then cook for 15 minutes longer.

3. Spread the spinach on a shallow platter. Spoon the lamb and orzo mixture over the spinach, then sprinkle with the crumbled feta.

LOW for 8–9 hours

For 4–6 servings:

1.2–1.5kg lamb shoulder chops

2 Tbsp plain flour

1 Tbsp olive or canola oil

2 medium onions

1kg all-purpose potatoes

1 x 400g can diced tomatoes in juice

½ cup red wine

2–3 cloves garlic

1 tsp dried basil

½ tsp dried marjoram

½–1 tsp salt

black pepper to taste

Italian-style Lamb Dinner

Shoulder chops are usually quite reasonably priced compared with other cuts of lamb and often seem to be on sale, making them an even better buy. They have a great flavour and come out wonderfully tender in this Italian-inspired one pot meal.

1. Sprinkle both sides of the chops with the flour. Heat the oil in a large non-stick frypan, then lightly brown the chops on both sides in batches.

2. While the chops brown, coat the inside of the bowl of a medium-to-large slow cooker with non-stick spray. Slice the onions, then sprinkle them into the slow cooker. Scrub the potatoes, cut each into 8 wedges and arrange them in a layer over the onions. Arrange the browned chops in a single layer (overlapping them if necessary) over the potatoes. Add the remaining ingredients to the frypan and stir to combine. Bring the mixture to the boil, then pour it evenly over the lamb.

3. Turn the slow cooker to LOW, cover and cook for 8–9 hours.

LOW for
6–8 hours

**Serves 8–10 as a starter or
4 as a main:**

Meatballs:

1 medium onion, roughly
chopped

2 thick slices bread, roughly
chopped or broken

500–600g minced lamb

1 tsp salt

1 Tbsp lemon juice

2 Tbsp canola oil

Sauce:

2 cloves garlic, chopped

1cm piece root ginger, peeled

1 tsp each ground cumin and
coriander

2 Tbsp each dark soy sauce
and lemon juice

½ tsp chilli powder
(or to taste)

¼ cup brown sugar

½ cup peanut butter

½ cup hot water

Sâté Meatballs

These meatballs may be made small and served with
dipping sauce as an appetiser. Alternatively, make
them larger and serve on rice with the sauce thinned
to gravy consistency.

1. Put the onion in a food processor, add the bread then process until
   the bread is in pea-size or smaller crumbs. Break the mince into golf
   ball-size pieces and add to the processor with the salt and lemon
   juice. Process in bursts until evenly mixed (don't process the
   mixture into a paste or the meatballs will be tough).

2. Heat the oil in a large frypan (or suitable slow cooker insert*).
   Working with wet hands, shape the mixture into 48 small balls or
   24 larger ones. Cook until they are lightly browned on all sides.

3. Coat the inside of the bowl of a medium-to-large slow cooker
   with non-stick spray. Transfer the browned meat balls to the
   slow cooker (or place the insert in the slow cooker).

4. To make the sauce, add the remaining ingredients to the cleaned
   food processor. Process until evenly combined, then pour the sauce
   over the meatballs.

5. Cover, turn to LOW and cook for 6–8 hours (if possible, stir once
   after 3–4 hours).

6. About 30 minutes before serving, check the consistency of the
   sauce and thin with some extra hot water if required. Taste and
   adjust the seasonings as required.

7. If serving the meatballs as an appetiser, spear each one with a
   toothpick. Serve on a shallow dish with some of the sauce on the
   side for dipping. For a main course, serve them on rice, with the
   sauce spooned over the top and a simple salad on the side.

* See the box on page 5.

LOW for
7–8 hours

For 4–6 servings:

2 Tbsp olive oil

500–600g diced lamb

1 large onion, quartered and sliced

300–400g golden kumara

300–400g parsnip

1 Tbsp cumin

1 Tbsp coriander

1 tsp turmeric

½ tsp allspice

5cm piece cinnamon stick

1 tsp minced red chilli or ½ tsp chilli powder

1 x 400g can diced tomatoes in juice

½–1 tsp salt

black pepper to taste

zest of 1 lemon

chopped parsley and/or coriander to garnish

Lamb and Kumara Tagine

Moroccan stews are called tagines, which is a reference to the containers they are cooked in. A tagine has a relatively wide shallow base with a distinctive tall, conical lid. The steam released during cooking condenses in the lid, then runs down the inside back into the stew, preventing it from drying out – the same principle as a slow cooker. This lamb tagine gives an interesting combination of flavours and textures.

1 Heat half the oil in a large frypan (or suitable slow cooker insert*) and lightly brown the lamb (best done in two batches unless using a large pan). Remove from the pan and set aside until required.

2 Coat the inside of the bowl of a large slow cooker with non-stick spray.

3 Heat the remaining oil in the pan (or slow cooker insert), then add the prepared vegetables and cook, stirring occasionally, until lightly browned. Stir in the spices and chilli and cook for 1–2 minutes longer, then add the tomatoes, salt and pepper.

4 Add the vegetable mixture and the lamb to the slow cooker and cover (or add the lamb to the vegetables, then place the insert in the slow cooker). Turn to LOW and cook for 7–8 hours or until the lamb is very tender.

5 Just before serving, stir in the lemon zest and adjust the seasonings if desired.

6 Serve over couscous or rice, garnished with a generous sprinkle of chopped parsley and/or coriander.

✳ See the box on page 5.

Pork

LOW for
6–8 hours

Kirsten's Pork and Pistachio Terrine

A terrine can be described as an upmarket meat loaf, usually sliced and eaten cold with pickles, potato salad, and a colourful salad alongside. It will keep well in the refrigerator for several days. Slice when you want it for easy summer entertaining.

For about 6 servings:

1 onion, finely chopped

400–500g pork or chicken mince

1 Tbsp finely chopped fresh sage leaves

1–2 Tbsp chopped parsley

2 Tbsp sherry

½ tsp salt

ground black pepper

10 whole sage or young bay leaves

about 10 strips thinly cut streaky bacon or prosciutto

300g pork belly strips

¼ cup shelled pistachio nuts

1. Mix together in a bowl the onion, mince, chopped sage and parsley, sherry, and salt and pepper.

2. Line a loaf tin with a strip of tinfoil with enough of an overhang to later fold over and cover the top of the terrine.

3. Arrange the whole sage leaves on the bottom of the tin, then line the sides and base with the streaky bacon or prosciutto, again allowing an overhang.

4. Spoon about a third of the mince mixture into the tin, then arrange half the pork belly strips on top lengthwise and sprinkle over half the nuts. Make two more layers, finishing with the final third of the mince mixture. Fold the ends of the streaky bacon over the top (it doesn't have to be too tidy as it will be the bottom of the terrine when it is unmoulded later).

5. Fold over the overhanging foil to cover the top of the terrine. Place the filled tin in the slow cooker on a small plate or trivet and pour in enough boiling water to come about halfway up the sides of the tin. Turn the slow cooker to LOW and cook for 6–8 hours.

6. Remove the terrine from the slow cooker and set it in a large pie dish or similar to catch any overflow from liquid formed during cooking. Choose an empty loaf tin about the same size as the terrine and position it on top. Fill the empty tin with several full cans from the store cupboard – the idea is to weigh down the terrine and keep the top flat.

7. Allow the terrine to cool, then refrigerate it overnight or until it is cold and set.

8. To serve, remove the foil and invert the loaf onto a plate. Cut into slices and serve with crusty bread, green pickles, and salad. When covered or stored in a plastic bag, the terrine will keep for several days in the refrigerator.

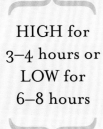

HIGH for
3–4 hours or
LOW for
6–8 hours

For 4–6 servings:

1 cup uncooked haricot beans (or 2 x 400g cans)

2 Tbsp olive or canola oil

1–1.2kg rolled pork loin or scotch roll

1 medium onion, quartered and sliced

2 cloves garlic, chopped

1 red pepper, deseeded and sliced

4 fresh sage leaves

2 bay leaves

1 x 400g can diced tomatoes in juice

¼ cup barbecue sauce

1 tsp salt

pepper to taste

Braised Pork with Beans

There's something about pork that makes it particularly good when served with beans. In this case the pork is effectively pot-roasted surrounded by a barbecue bean mixture – a very delicious combination indeed.

1. If you are using uncooked beans, soak them overnight then put them in the slow cooker and cover with 4 cups of hot water. Cover and cook on HIGH for 3–4 hours or until the beans are tender. Drain and set aside.

2. Heat the oil in a large frypan. Add the pork and brown on all sides.

3. Coat the inside of the bowl of a medium slow cooker with non-stick spray. Transfer the browned pork to the slow cooker.

4. Add the onion, garlic and red pepper to the frypan, and cook, stirring frequently, until soft. Stir in the sage and bay leaves and cook for 1 minute longer, then add the tomatoes and juice, barbecue sauce, and salt and pepper to taste. Gently stir in the drained beans, then bring the mixture to the boil.

5. Pour the bean mixture over the pork in the slow cooker, cover and turn to HIGH. Cook for 3–4 hours or LOW for 6–8 hours.

6. Serve with a green salad or lightly cooked vegetables and some crusty bread on the side.

LOW for
7–9 hours

For 4–6 servings:

1–1.2kg pork, diced

¼ cup wine vinegar

3 bay leaves

1 cinnamon stick, about
5cm long

4–6 cardamom pods, crushed

2 Tbsp canola oil

2 medium onions, diced

4 cloves garlic, chopped

2cm piece root ginger, finely
chopped

2 tsp each ground cumin,
coriander and mustard seeds

½–1 tsp chilli powder

1 tsp each ground fenugreek,
turmeric, black pepper and
salt

500g all-purpose or boiling
potatoes

Pork Vindaloo

Potatoes sometimes get an unusual texture when cooked in the slow cooker, so we prefer to cook the potatoes for this vindaloo separately, then add them during the last half hour or so of cooking (which also helps thicken the curry).

1. Coat the inside of the bowl of a medium slow cooker with non-stick spray. Put the diced pork in the slow cooker followed by the vinegar, bay leaves, cinnamon stick and crushed cardamom pods. Stir to combine, then set the slow cooker to LOW.

2. Heat the oil in a large frypan over a medium-high heat. Add the diced onion and cook, stirring occasionally, until it has softened. Stir in the garlic and ginger and continue to cook until the onion begins to brown. Measure in the spices and salt and pepper and stir-fry for about 1 minute longer.

3. Stir the onion-spice mixture into the pork in the slow cooker, then cover and cook on LOW for 7–9 hours.

4. About an hour before you want to eat, peel the potatoes, cut them into 2–3cm cubes and boil in a pot on the stove until cooked through. Drain well and stir into the curry. Put the lid back on and cook for about 30 minutes.

5. Serve with steamed rice and a simple salad or raita. Naan bread and/or poppadums also make ideal accompaniments.

Vegetarian

HIGH for
3–4 hours

For 6 servings:

2 x 400g cans diced
tomatoes in juice

1 tsp each dried basil and
garlic salt

½ tsp dried oregano

½ tsp pepper

500g frozen spinach, thawed

250g cottage cheese

½ cup grated parmesan
cheese

¼ tsp freshly grated nutmeg

1 cup grated tasty cheese

250g dried lasagne

Sauce:

3 Tbsp butter

3 Tbsp plain flour

½ tsp salt

pepper to taste

1½ cups milk

1 cup grated tasty cheese

1 large egg

Spinach and Cottage Cheese Lasagne

This lasagne requires very little preparation. It only takes about 10 minutes to assemble, then you simply turn on the slow cooker and leave it for a few hours. Perfect!

1. Coat the inside of the bowl of a medium-sized slow cooker with non-stick spray.

2. Tip the diced tomatoes and juice into a medium-size bowl. Add the basil, garlic salt, oregano and pepper and stir to combine.

3. Lightly squeeze the thawed spinach to get rid of some of the liquid. Place the squeezed spinach in a separate bowl and add the cottage cheese, parmesan cheese and nutmeg. Stir to combine.

4. Arrange a layer of lasagne sheets in the slow cooker. Pour in half the tomato mixture and spread it over the lasagne. Sprinkle with half of the grated tasty cheese. Add another layer of lasagne, then spread the spinach mixture over it. Cover the spinach with a final layer of lasagne, then pour and spread over the remaining tomato mixture. Sprinkle with the remaining grated cheese.

5. To make the sauce, melt the butter in a medium-size pot. Sprinkle in the flour and stir for about 1 minute. Add salt and pepper to taste, then pour in half the milk. Whisk until there are no lumps and the sauce has thickened and come to the boil. Allow the sauce to boil for about 1 minute, then add the remaining milk. Whisk until smooth, then again bring the sauce to the boil. Remove from the heat, stir in the grated cheese, and keep stirring while you add the egg.

6. Pour the sauce over the lasagne, then dust the top lightly with paprika. Set the slow cooker to HIGH, cover and cook for 3–4 hours.

7. Cut into portions and carefully lift out using a wide fish slice. Crusty or garlic bread and a crisp green salad on the side make this a delicious meal.

Kirsten's Pasta Bake

This is a really useful way of making a pasta bake when the oven is being used for other things. Kirsten takes the prepared mixture in the slow cooker to work where she cooks it on LOW for 4–6 hours, but it can be cooked on HIGH for 1 hour from room temperature or 2 hours on HIGH if has been refrigerated. Although the crumb topping is not crunchy, no one ever complains!

To make it go further among her colleagues, Kirsten adds broccoli or cauliflower florets to the pasta.

Serves 6–8 as main dish or more as a side dish:

500g chunky pasta shapes

1 cup small broccoli or cauliflower florets or a mixture of both, optional

Sauce:

2 x 400g cans chopped tomatoes in juice

300ml cream or 250g light sour cream

2 cups tasty grated cheese

1 tsp sugar

1 tsp salt

freshly ground black pepper

½ cup fresh basil leaves, roughly torn, or ¼ cup chopped fresh parsley and 1 Tbsp dried oregano

Topping:

¼ cup dry or golden breadcrumbs

½ cup grated cheese, ideally parmesan

fresh herbs, optional

1 Cook the pasta in plenty of salted water in a pot on the stove until just tender (choose the shortest cooking time from the options on the packet). Drain the pasta and put into the slow cooker. If including broccoli or cauliflower, add to the boiling pasta in the last minute to blanch.

2 While the pasta cooks, combine the tomatoes, cream, the first measure of grated cheese, sugar, salt, pepper, and basil in the food processor. Process until well mixed. Alternatively, finely chop the herbs and mix in a large bowl with the other ingredients. Tip the mixture over the pasta in the slow cooker and stir to coat. (It will be a bit sloppy).

3 To make the topping, combine the breadcrumbs with the second measure of cheese and the herbs, if using, in the uncleaned food processor and briefly process (or combine the cheese with the finely chopped herbs and breadcrumbs in a small bowl). Sprinkle the topping over the pasta.

4 The mixture can be refrigerated overnight, then cooked on LOW for 4–6 hours or HIGH for 2–3 hours.

LOW for 6–7
hours, then
HIGH for
30 minutes

For 6 servings:

2 Tbsp olive or canola oil

1 medium onion, diced

2 cloves garlic, chopped

250g large brown mushrooms, sliced

2 cups pearl barley

1 tsp dried thyme

½ tsp dried marjoram

4–5 cups vegetable or chicken stock

¼ cup sherry

½–1 tsp salt

½ cup cream

½ cup grated parmesan cheese

½–1 cup frozen peas or beans

black pepper to taste

Mushroom and Barley Risotto

This isn't a true risotto – not only because the texture is a bit different, but pearl barley stands up better to slow cooking than rice. It makes a substantial meal on its own or makes a good side dish.

1. Coat the inside of the bowl of a large slow cooker with non-stick spray.

2. Heat the oil in a large frypan (or suitable slow cooker insert*). Add the onion and garlic and cook, stirring frequently to prevent browning, until the onion has softened.

3. Gently stir in the sliced mushrooms and cook for a few minutes longer until the mushrooms just begin to wilt. Add the pearl barley and dried herbs, then stir to lightly coat the barley with the oil.

4. Transfer the onion, mushroom and barley mixture to the slow cooker (or place the insert in the slow cooker). Pour in 4 cups of the stock and add the sherry and ½ teaspoon of salt. Turn to LOW, cover and cook for 6–7 hours.

5. Turn the slow cooker to HIGH and add the cream, parmesan cheese and frozen peas or beans. Stir to combine. The mixture should be runny enough so a spoonful just holds its shape but if it appears dry, add about ¼ cup at a time of the remaining stock. Cook for 30 minutes longer, then season to taste with the remaining salt and the black pepper.

6. Serve as a main course with a salad or vegetables on the side, or as a side dish.

✳ See the box on page 5.

LOW for
6–8 hours

Spiced Chickpea and Butternut Tagine

You'll need to soak the chickpeas overnight before making this easy tagine. A delicious vegetarian meal, it's quite substantial but still light enough to serve on a warmer evening.

For 4 servings:

2 Tbsp olive oil

1 large onion, quartered and sliced

3 cloves garlic, chopped

600g peeled and deseeded butternut

2 tsp cumin seed

1 tsp each paprika and turmeric

5cm piece cinnamon stick

½ tsp minced red chilli, optional

1 x 400g can diced tomatoes in juice

2 x 400g cans chickpeas

zest and juice of ½ lemon

1–2 tsp honey

½–1 tsp salt

pepper to taste

1–2 Tbsp each chopped parsley and coriander

1. Coat the inside of the bowl of a medium slow cooker with non-stick spray.

2. Heat the oil over a medium-high heat in a large frypan (or in a suitable slow cooker insert*). Add the onion and garlic to the pan and cook, stirring occasionally, for about 5 minutes or until the onion is soft and turning clear.

3. Cut the butternut into 2cm cubes and add to the pan. Stir in the spices and cook for 1–2 minutes longer, then add the tomatoes in their juice. Bring the mixture to the boil, then transfer it to the slow cooker (or transfer the insert into the slow cooker).

4. Drain the chickpeas, then add to the slow cooker. Turn to LOW, cover and cook for 6–8 hours or until the chickpeas are tender.

5. Stir in the lemon zest and juice, honey, salt and pepper to taste and most of the parsley and chopped coriander, reserving a little to garnish.

6. Serve with rice or couscous garnished with the remaining herbs.

✳ See the box on page 5.

Vegetables & Sides

HIGH for
4 hours

For 4 servings:

1kg potatoes, scrubbed

2–3 tsp canola or olive oil

100g bacon, rind removed

¼ cup milk

1 x 425g can condensed
cream of chicken soup

1–2 cups grated tasty cheese

2–3 Tbsp dried golden
breadcrumbs

½ tsp paprika

Cheesy Potato Bake

This cheesy potato mixture is good with any unaccompanied cooked meat, i.e. without a sauce or gravy. The potatoes should be cooked until they are just tender before they are put in the slow cooker with the remaining ingredients. (See below for pre-cooking the potatoes.)

1. Coat the inside of the bowl of a medium slow cooker with non-stick spray and turn to HIGH.

2. Cut the scrubbed potatoes crosswise into 7mm slices. Place in a microwave-proof plastic bag and add the oil. Loosely close the bag, then gently knead until all the potato slices are covered with a thin film of oil. Microwave at HIGH (100%) power for 12–15 minutes or until tender.

3. Chop the bacon into small pieces, and put them aside, then mix together the milk and cream of chicken soup in a bowl or jug.

4. Put one-third of the microwaved potatoes in the slow cooker, then sprinkle half the bacon over them. Drizzle over one-third of the milk and soup mixture, then sprinkle over one-third of the cheese.

5. Repeat with one-third of the potatoes, the remaining bacon, another third of the creamy mixture and half of the remaining cheese.

6. Make a final layer with the remaining potatoes, soup mixture and the cheese, then sprinkle with the breadcrumbs and paprika. Cook on HIGH for 4 hours.

7. Serve, using a saucer to lift out each portion.

LOW for
4–5 hours

Creamy Rice and Vegetables

This side dish makes a good accompaniment for barbecued chicken or sausages, etc. It is surprising what a difference a little cream makes to the rice mixture. Any leftover mixture may be refrigerated and reheated in a microwave oven the next day.

For about 4 servings:

25g butter

1 cup long grain rice

2 carrots

2 cups boiling water

2 tsp instant chicken stock powder

¼ cup cream

3–4 spring onions, finely chopped, or ½ cup finely chopped parsley

1 Coat the inside of the bowl of a medium-sized slow cooker with non-stick spray and turn to LOW. Put the butter followed by the rice into the slow cooker.

2 Using a sharp knife, cut the carrots lengthwise into long thin strips, then crosswise into small cubes about the size of frozen peas. Add to the slow cooker.

3 Pour in the boiling water, then stir in the chicken stock. Add the cream and mix everything together until the butter has melted.

4 Cover and cook on LOW for 4–5 hours until the rice is tender and all the liquid is absorbed.

5 Just before serving, evenly fold the spring onion or parsley through the rice mixture.

LOW for about
6 hours

Pickled Red Cabbage

Pickled red cabbage is interesting and different! It will keep in the refrigerator for 3–4 days. You may like to serve it, as we do, with barbecued sausages. Although we usually reheat it before we serve it, some people like it cold too.

We don't put it in sandwiches or filled rolls which will be left to stand for some time before they are eaten, because the red colour comes out into the bread, but it is a good addition to sandwiches or rolls which will be eaten straight away.

Makes 4–6 servings:

500g red cabbage (1 small or ½ large)

2 Tbsp brown sugar

3 Tbsp red wine or malt vinegar

2 Tbsp sweet chilli sauce

2 apples, preferably tart

1. Coat the inside of the bowl of a medium slow cooker with non-stick spray and turn to LOW.

2. Quarter the red cabbage and remove and discard the tough outer leaves and the solid core. Thinly shred the cabbage and put it in the slow cooker.

3. Add the next three ingredients to the slow cooker and mix thoroughly through the cabbage.

4. Cut the unpeeled apples into quarters and remove the cores. Cut each quarter into thin slices, then matchstick strips. To avoid the apple strips browning, toss them through the cabbage mixture immediately.

5. Cook on LOW for about 6 hours.

6. Serve immediately or put it into jars with lids and refrigerate for up to 1 week.

Something Sweet

Spiced Apple Crumble

The topping on an apple crumble cooked in a slow cooker is not as crisp as that of a baked apple crumble, but it is still very good, and has a lovely flavour. To save time and money, we don't peel the apples before we slice them into the slow cooker – the skins become very soft as they cook.

For 4 servings:

800g apples, preferably braeburn or granny smith

pinch of ground cloves and mixed spice, optional

¼ cup orange juice or diluted lemon cordial

Topping:

½ cup flour

½ cup brown sugar

1 tsp mixed spice

50g cold butter, cut into cubes

½ cup rolled oats

1. Coat the inside of the bowl of a medium-sized slow cooker with non-stick spray and turn to HIGH.

2. Working with one at a time and using a sharp knife, cut the apples into quarters. Remove the core and any seeds using a V-shaped cut. Cut each unpeeled quarter crosswise into thin slices.

3. Spread half of the apple slices in the base of the slow cooker bowl and sprinkle with the cloves and mixed spice, if using. Dribble about 1 tablespoon of juice or cordial over the apple to stop it browning. Make a second layer with the remaining apple and sprinkle over the rest of the juice or cordial.

4. Firmly press down on the apple layers with your hand. Place a sheet of baking paper or foil over the apple, cover and cook on HIGH for 2 hours.

5. Towards the end of the cooking time, combine the flour, brown sugar, mixed spice and butter into a food processor, and process until the butter is in small pieces. Stir in the rolled oats without breaking them up.

6. Remove the lid of the slow cooker and lift out the sheet of baking paper or foil. Sprinkle the oat mixture over the apple, then cover and cook on HIGH for another 2 hours, then turn off the power and remove the lid so the topping will become crisper. (If you are not planning to eat the crumble within an hour, leave the uncovered mixture to stand in the cooker turned to WARM or LOW).

7. To serve, lift out portions with a saucer. Serve warm with whipped cream, yoghurt or ice cream.

To make 3–4 cups:

1kg apples

zest of 1 orange, grated

juice of 1 orange

2 whole cinnamon sticks

1 vanilla pod, optional

¼–½ cup sugar

Spiced Apple Purée

Can you believe that it's possible to cook apples with their skins on in a slow cooker, then process the cooked fruit in a food processor with absolutely no sign of any apple skin?

Alison's favourite way of enjoying this spiced purée is to put a few large spoonfuls in a bowl with a scoop of boysenberry ice cream and some of her favourite crunchy muesli. She says she can happily eat this mixture at any time of the day or night. Try it, and see for yourself!

1 Coat the inside of the bowl of a medium slow cooker with non-stick spray.

2 Quarter the apples, cut out the core, then slice each quarter lengthwise in half, then crosswise to make 16 chunks per apple. Put them into the slow cooker and turn to HIGH.

3 Zest then juice the orange. Sprinkle the orange juice and grated zest over the apple (don't be tempted to add any other liquid). Add the cinnamon sticks and the vanilla pod, if using. Cover and cook on HIGH for about 4 hours.

4 Remove the cinnamon sticks and the vanilla pod from the slow cooker. Gently wash them and put them aside to dry for reuse if desired.

5 Tip the apple mixture into a food processor with ¼ cup of the sugar and purée. Process until smooth, then taste and add more sugar if necessary.

6 Serve as desired and store any leftover purée in a lidded container for 3–4 days in the fridge.

HIGH for
1–2 hours

For 4 servings:

¼ cup seedless raisins

¼ cup dark rum

2 Tbsp butter

¼ cup brown sugar

¼ tsp grated nutmeg

¼ tsp ground cinnamon

4 slightly under-ripe bananas

Hot Bananas with Rum and Raisins

A real treat for those who like the flavour of rum, this dessert should be eaten as soon as the bananas are cooked because that's when their colour and texture are at their best.

1 Combine the raisins and rum in a small microwave-proof container, cover loosely and cook in the microwave on HIGH (100% power) for 1 minute.

2 Coat the inside of the bowl of a medium slow cooker with non-stick spray and turn to HIGH. Add the butter, brown sugar, nutmeg and cinnamon to the slow cooker and allow the butter to melt.

3 Diagonally slice the bananas into 4–5 pieces each and stir into the mixture along with the rum and raisins.

4 Cook for 1–2 hours on HIGH (the bananas will go very soft if left for the longer time).

Carrot Loaf

We are always surprised to see what good results we get from a sweet loaf baked in a slow cooker. The texture is excellent and we find that it tastes just as good 3–4 days after cooking as it did the day it was made. We make this loaf in an 11 x 22cm, 5-cup capacity metal loaf tin. This size tin fits nicely in our large slow cooker.

For a 5-cup loaf:

¾ cup sugar

¼ cup milk

½ cup canola oil

2 large eggs

1 tsp salt

1½ cups grated raw carrot

1½ cups plain flour

2 tsp cinnamon

1 tsp baking powder

½ tsp baking soda

1. Measure the first five ingredients into a large bowl and beat with an egg beater until thoroughly blended. Mix the carrot through the beaten mixture. Sift the remaining ingredients into the bowl and use a flexible stirrer to mix everything together.

2. Coat the inside of the loaf tin with non-stick spray or line the bottom and long sides of the tin with a strip of baking paper. Spoon the mixture into the loaf tin, levelling off the top.

3. Stand the uncovered loaf in the slow cooker. Put on the lid and cook on HIGH for 1½ hours or until a skewer inserted into the middle comes out clean.

4. Remove the loaf in its tin from the slow cooker and leave to stand for about 10 minutes. When ready to turn out, run a knife between the loaf in the unlined tin, then carefully unmould it. Allow to cool, then store any leftovers in a plastic bag in the fridge.

HIGH for
3–3½ hours

For 6 servings:

100g butter

½ cup (100g) chocolate chips

½ cup sugar

2 large eggs

4 heaped Tbsp raspberry jam

1 tsp vanilla essence

¾ cup (100g) flour

½ tsp baking powder

Raspberry and Chocolate Brownie Pudding

While this brownie-based dessert isn't like a conventional baked brownie, the raspberry jam gives it a delicious twist. Serve it topped with a little chocolate or raspberry sauce and some ice cream on the side.

1 Heat the butter and chocolate chips together in a medium-size pot over a low heat, stirring until smooth. Remove from the heat and stir in the sugar, eggs, jam and vanilla essence. Sift in the flour and baking powder, then stir until combined.

2 Thoroughly non-stick spray 2 x 800g empty cans or a 7-cup capacity loaf tin. Pour half the batter into each tin or the loaf tin, then cover the top/s tightly with baking paper, securing with a rubber band.

3 Place the tin/s in the slow cooker and pour in 2–3cm of hot water. Turn to HIGH, cover and cook for 3–3½ hours or until a skewer poked into the centre comes out clean.

4 Remove from the slow cooker and allow to cool on a rack for 5 minutes before turning out. If they seem sticky, run a knife or spatula round the outside edge first. Allow to cool for a few minutes longer before cutting.

5 Serve warm with ice cream and a squirt of chocolate or raspberry ice cream topping.

For 4 servings:

¼ cup sago

1¼ cups hot water

500–600g red plums

1 tsp ground cinnamon

¼ tsp ground cloves

½ cup sugar

Spiced Plum Sago

This mixture is really delicious! You can use whichever variety of plum you like, but we particularly recommend a variety called Louise, which is the shape and size of an egg. When ripe, this plum is as red inside as it is outside.

1. Coat the inside of the bowl of a medium-sized slow cooker with non-stick spray and turn to HIGH.

2. Evenly sprinkle the sago into the slow cooker, then add the hot water, stirring to avoid lumps forming.

3. Cut each plum in half and remove the stone, then cut in half again to make 4 pieces. Add the quartered plums to the slow cooker, sprinkle with the cinnamon and ground cloves and stir to mix well.

4. Cover and cook on HIGH for about 2 hours until the sago is transparent.

5. Sprinkle the sugar over the clear sago mixture and stir gently so the plums keep their shape. Serve with cream or yoghurt while the mixture is warm.

LOW for about
9 hours

For 2–3 servings:

½ cup rolled oats

¼ tsp salt

2 cups cold water

about ½ cup dried fruit, e.g.
chopped dried apricots,
chopped dates, dried
cranberries, blueberries,
sultanas and/or raisins

Fruity Porridge

This recipe is particularly useful for people who don't function too well in the early morning. All they need to do is assemble the ingredients in the slow cooker after dinner and turn it to LOW just before they go to bed. Then, hey presto – next morning it's just a matter of stirring the porridge and spooning as much as each person likes into a bowl and adding some milk, cream or yoghurt – and perhaps a sprinkling of sugar. It's a good, interesting and substantial breakfast that can be made with your own modifications, e.g. more or less liquid, more or less diced fruit, or different dried fruits, and so on.

1. Select a bowl that will hold at least 4 cups of liquid and which will fit in your slow cooker. Position the bowl in the slow cooker and pour water around it to come two-thirds up the sides.

2. Coat the inside of the empty bowl with non-stick spray. Combine the oats, salt and cold water in the bowl, stir to mix then stir in your choice of dried fruit (chop large pieces of dried fruit in half).

3. Cover the bowl with a plate to fit, then position the lid on top of the slow cooker or put a piece of aluminium foil with the edges loosely pressed down, over the bowl. Turn to LOW and leave overnight. The next morning, sprinkle each portion with white or brown sugar and add a little milk, cream or yoghurt.

Index

Knives etc., by Mail Order

For about 20 years Alison has imported her favourite, very sharp kitchen knives from Switzerland. They keep their edges well, are easy to sharpen, a pleasure to use, and make excellent gifts.

VEGETABLE KNIFE $8.00

Ideal for cutting and peeling vegetables, these knives have a straight edged 85mm blade and black (dishwasher-proof) nylon handle. Each knife comes in an individual plastic sheath.

BONING/UTILITY KNIFE $9.50

Excellent for boning chicken and other meats, and/or for general kitchen duties. Featuring a 103mm blade that curves to a point and a dishwasher-proof, black nylon handle. Each knife comes in a plastic sheath.

SERRATED KNIFE $9.50

These knives are unbelievably useful. They are perfect for cutting cooked meats, ripe fruit and vegetables, and slicing bread and baking. Treated carefully, these blades stay sharp for years. The serrated 110mm blade is rounded at the end with a black (dishwasher-proof) nylon handle and each knife comes in an individual plastic sheath.

THREE-PIECE SET $22.00

This three-piece set includes a vegetable knife, a serrated knife (as described above) and a right-handed potato peeler with a matching black handle, presented in a white plastic wallet.

GIFT BOXED KNIFE SET $44.00

This set contains five knives plus a matching right-handed potato peeler. There is a straight bladed vegetable knife and a serrated knife (as above), as well as a handy 85mm serrated blade vegetable knife, a small (85mm) utility knife with a pointed tip and a smaller (85mm) serrated knife. These elegantly presented sets make ideal gifts.

SERRATED CARVING KNIFE $28.50

This fabulous knife cuts beautifully and is a pleasure to use; it's ideal for carving or cutting fresh bread. The 21cm serrated blade does not require sharpening. Once again the knife has a black moulded, dishwasher safe handle and comes in a plastic sheath.

COOK'S KNIFE $35.00

An excellent all-purpose kitchen knife. With a well balanced 19cm wedge-shaped blade and a contoured black nylon handle, these knives make short work of slicing and chopping, and have come out on top of their class in several comparative tests. Each dishwasher-safe knife comes with its own plastic sheath.

VICTORINOX MULTIPURPOSE KITCHEN SHEARS $29.50

Every kitchen should have a pair of these! With their comfortable nylon handles and sharp blades these quality shears make short work of everything from cutting a piece of string or sheet of paper to jointing a whole chicken. Note: Black handle only.

STEEL $20.00

These steels have a 20cm 'blade' and measure 33cm in total. With its matching black handle the steel is an ideal companion for your own knives, or as a gift. Alison gets excellent results using these steels. N.B. Not for use with serrated knives.

PROBUS SPREADER/SCRAPER $7.50

After her knives, these are the most used tools in Alison's kitchen! With a comfortable plastic handle, metal shank and flexible plastic blade (suitable for use on non-stick surfaces), these are excellent for mixing muffin batters, stirring and scraping bowls, spreading icings, turning pikelets etc., etc...

NON-STICK LINERS

Re-usable SureBrand PTFE non-stick liners are another essential kitchen item – they really help avoid the frustration of stuck-on baking, roasting or frying. Once you've used them, you'll wonder how you did without!

Round tin liner	(for 15-23cm tins)	$6.95
	(for 23-30cm tins)	$9.95
Square tin liner	(for 15-23cm tins)	$6.95
	(for 23-30cm tins)	$9.95
Ring tin liner	(for 23cm tins)	$7.50
Baking sheet liner	(33x44cm)	$14.50
Barbeque liner	(Heavy duty 33x44cm)	$18.50
Frypan liner	(Heavy duty round 30cm)	$11.50

All prices include GST. Prices current at time of publishing, subject to change without notice. Please add $5.00 post & packing to any order (any number of items).

Make cheques payable to Alison Holst Mail Orders and post to:

Alison Holst Mail Orders
FREEPOST 124807
PO Box 17016
Wellington

Or visit us at www.holst.co.nz